DIARY O
HONEY BEE

DIARY OF A HONEYBEE

I am a beekeeper.
My bees make honey for me to sell.
They collect it from flowers.

In spring, I look into my hives
every few days
to make sure the bees are growing
and working hard.
I keep a diary of what I see.

DAY 1

Today there are fresh eggs
in the bottom of the wax cells.
The queen bee laid them – one in each cell.

DAY 2

The eggs are hatching into little grubs
called larvae.
The nurse bees feed bee jelly
and honey to the grubs.
The bee jelly comes from a gland
in the bee's head.

DAY 9

The larvae are changing into pupae.
The nurse bees stop feeding them
and close the cell with a wax lid.

DAY 21

Something is eating its way
out of the top of the cell.
It is a new worker bee.

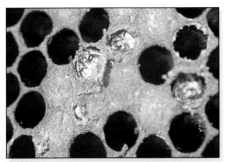 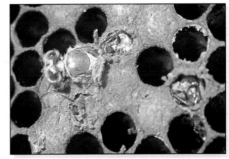

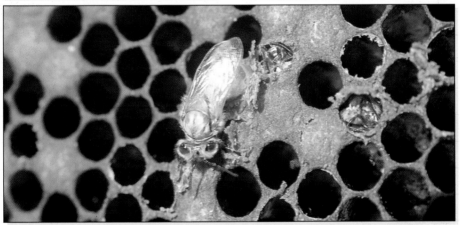

At first it walks around doing nothing.
Then it helps the other young bees
to clean the empty cells,
ready for more eggs.

DAY 24

Now the young bees are allowed
to do nurse duty.

They feed the very young grubs.

DAY 34

The worker bees are now old enough to make wax.
The wax comes from glands
under their abdomens.
The worker bees build comb cells out of
the wax and help store the honey in them.

DAY 39

Now worker bees are put on guard duty
at the door of the hive.
They make sure no wasps or mice
come in to steal honey.
They also fan with their wings on hot days
to help cool the hive.
Some do hive cleaning duty.

DAY 42

At last, the bees are old enough
to be field bees.
They fly around the fields and forests
collecting nectar and pollen from flowers
to bring back to the hive.
They make about a hundred trips a day.
When they bring nectar back to the hive,
the hive bees make it into honey
by chewing it and warming it.
If a field bee finds new flowers,
she dances on the honeycomb
to tell the other field bees where to go.

14

INTERESTING FACTS ABOUT BEES

1. A worker bee lives for about 45 days.

2. Worker bees have special hairs on their legs to brush pollen from flowers.

3. Bees pollinate a wide range of fruit, vegetables, and forest plants.

4. Worker bees fly about 25 km an hour (15 mph) and will fly up to 800 km (500 mi) in their lifetime.

5. Every day, a worker bee makes about enough honey to cover a pin-head.

6. The queen bee lives for about three years and is the mother of all the bees in the hive. You can recognize the queen because she is bigger and has a longer body.

15

GLOSSARY

ABDOMEN	stomach
GLAND	an organ in the body that makes chemicals
HONEYCOMB	the structure the bees make to hold their honey and eggs
LARVAE	grubs
NECTAR	sugary solution
POLLEN	yellow dust-like substance found in flowers
PUPA	the sleeping and changing form of an insect
WAX	a dull yellow substance secreted by bees to make their cells